1

2

Sea Sonnets

by David Hirzel

For Alice

First published in 2009 by
Terra Nova Press, P. O. Box 1808, Pacifica, CA 94044

Printed in the United States of America

SECOND EDITION 2013

Author contact: *info@terra-nova-press.com*
Website: *www.davidhirzel.net*

Contents

Part One: Boats

Part Two: Waters

Part Three: Ships

Part Four: Navigation

Part One: Boats

Catboat, Sunset

The twilight settles, purple, gold. The gusts
have died away, the tide's slow flood
moves nothing. The crew (one man) trusts,
not thinking on it, how his captain's good
sense of hull, rig, tide, wind, keel,
will be enough to bring this catboat, small craft,
in with not one breath of wind to fill
the slack canvas. The two sit right aft,
hand to tiller, hand to sheet, the channel markers
pass in utter silence. Ghosting, a wraith
homeward bound, the catboat's in her berth by dark.
It's the unseen forces that drive us, or perhaps they pull,
and all that's needed is confidence or faith.
The sail, even slack, is never less than full.

Catboat Closehauled

This drop-keeled boat's a remarkable thing:
one sail scarce bigger than a bedsheet, gaffed
to a tabernacle mast, an upright canvas wing,
the catboat's sole propulsion, fore-and-aft.
Wind astern, she goes on a broad reach,
waltzing downwind in a simple dance,
but head-to-wind, now that's the thing to teach;
it counters a landsman's reason and his sense.
Here's the rule: bear up to windward till the leech
just flutters; ease off. Mind how she heels.
A shift of wind abeam could swamp us. Don't think.
You need no more than notice how she feels,
and act on it, trusting; she's not content to drift,
unless you let her, or run aground, or sink.

A Dory

We were abroad, rowing on the Bay.
Two people, four oars, one dory, and nothing else beside.
The morning's gentle sun gave way
to cloud and rain, and wind against the rising tide.
The wind picked up, sweeping past our mark.
We made no headway; the boat would not be steered.
She spun on an axis, leapt, plunged, veered—
but shipped no water. She floated like a cork.
The dory by reputation will not capsize.
You can put your faith in that. Her sloped gunwales
turn away whitecaps; she remains afloat
in any weather. Let the tempest rise,
and rising push up towering swells,
do what it may. Nothing overturns this boat.

Part Two: Waters

Aubade

After a silent sailing down the bay
alive with sea-life, a million birds afloat
and calling after herring roe, we're under way
upwind; the noisy motor drives our little boat.
We're on to other music. The gathered crowd
sings the old sea-songs into the night
if not melodically, then loud.
Then pops a champagne cork. In time the dawn
to birdsong shows her quiet light;
we lay entwined, and call each others' names.
Above all these sounds there will be one
I'll carry with me always in the deep
pocket of my heart, as your every breath becomes
slower, deeper, until I know you safe asleep.

Rivers

From my window I can see each
great river of the world, all harbors, bays,
estuaries. The mighty Hudson's reach
past New York's fingered wharves, the ways
of Hamburg, Belfast, Newport News,
Pearl's sunken caldera, Yokohama's inland sea,
Panama's lifts, Colorado's despondent sloughs,
Ganges, Rhine—they all flow here to me.
These are highway, field, freight and sustenance.
The sea absorbs all Columbia's epic flood,
with all the rest, and does not rise. A fall
comes only with the tide's celestial dance.
All water is one great pulsing blood
that, one way or another, feeds us all.

Maury's Button

She has a button salved from Maury's coat
and handed down, a brass anchor on
an ebon disc, hung on a golden chain
she wears at certain sea-times round her throat.
Matthew Fontane Maury (for those who ask)
for years studied the logs of ocean ships for clues
to the probable currents of wind. This task,
fulfilled, published, put by the wise to use,
shows how the powers that drive us are always present,
invisible and predictable as the trade
winds, the light airs of the doldrums, the swirled
cyclonic gales reversing on us. His intent
is manifest, that simple study of the book he made
can guide us in our passage through this world.

These Uncharted Seas

These blue sheets might be uncharted seas
we sail upon. We rise and fall, tossed
wave upon wave, and on each crest seize
another sun-sight to prove we are not lost,
though (dare I say it) we are abandoned here
and cast thus away, we will not be found.
There are no latitudes marked upon this sphere,
no equator binds this world around.
Like Bounty's roaming hands, we find
seclusion here abroad on the pillowed deep,
to come ashore with unshackled passions fed,
and worldly cares left somewhere far behind.
Our vessel burned to the waterline, we sleep,
our whole globe encompassed in this bed.

Tidal Falls

In Maine, the shadow of the singing bridge spans
a tidal rapid. Over each bank the arching pines
bear witness: salt water runs in a rush
upstream, tumbling over stones just below
the animate surface. A pause, then fresh
from its natural source resumes its flow,
to cleanse, heal, revive, replenish
the brackish stream, the thirsting deer,
the fainting flesh, the wounded heart, the salt blood.
Invisibly over our heads the moon's hand
leads this eternal dance, the ebb-and-flood
celestial pulse, the push-pull-push
made manifest, and visible here,
reconciled with faith, and understood.

Part Three: Ships

Dawn Watch

The sea's like hammered silver, a heaving wedge
brilliant in moonlight, dazzling the eye
outward to the night sky's razor edge,
tossing waves beneath the deep indigo sky.
This ship's a roller; the arc of the mast sweeps
the stars from forty-five degrees. The watch
on deck's busy all night, that below sleeps,
or tries to. The captain strikes a match.
Nothing's to be heard but the variable slap
of cross-sea on bow, the hastening surge
of water alongside, the jib's intermittent flap,
too close to wind. Venus and Mercury launch their show;
moonlight, twilight, dawn light merge.
The dawn watch ends. The seamen go below.

Course Steered

Steering the course ordered is the hardest thing to learn.
Vehicles on land respond in a given way
with a corresponding logic to each turn
of the wheel. Not so this vessel under weigh.
Two full turns here have the desired effect
one full minute from now, and now—before you go
well beyond your intended bearing—you must correct,
anticipating all. There's more you need to know:
she's heavy aft; the wind varies for speed
and direction; the swell off the starboard quarter will
heel and spin her, but she comes back. Don't chase
the compass this dark night. What you need's
to trust what you can't see, the wind on your face,
the ship in the water, your own hands on the wheel.

Rhumb Line

The helmsman's given compass bearings to keep—
one, "course ordered" by the Captain, another to steer—
"course steered", by the Mate, and the ship
has her own ideas, subject to the wind's veer.
A designated hand takes the navigator's part,
notes the GPS at the turn of each hour religiously,
pencils the vessel's exact position on the chart.
So in angular segments she seems to move across the sea.
The log line's a different measure of distance run.
Courses ordered, steered, log line, current, tide, wind,
the Captain's careful judgment, dead-reckoning, however
         sound,
are all but half-truths we interpret and refine.
It's the rhumbline connecting our days in a straight line
that tells the overall tale of our passage, where we've been,
how carefully we've steered the course, where we're bound.

Forward Lookout

Under all plain sail, a ship races forward.
The lookout, one lone sailor taking his place
at the fo'c'sle-head, arcs heavenward
on the tumbled swell, falls from such grace.
Steady there, he stands, the ship's own eyes,
scans from beam to beam the flat ocean-world, halved
by the ship's own axes. In all he surveys,
no danger lies ahead, abeam, abaft.
No matter that the blue horizon's clear,
that nothing's in sight on all the heaving sea--
the vigil's not for one second let to fail.
Others mind the compass, tend the sail.
Each is shaped to duty. These eyes must see
all that the helm cannot, who's tasked to steer.

Anchor Watch

The hook's down, well dug-in to the chosen ground
dedicated to anchorage; the scope's out, the chain's
two shots an unseen spring, the mooring's sound—
or seems to be. With sail in, way stopped, she spins
on the pivot of her anchor, head-to-wind.
But for two hands, the watch is sent below.
One keeps land bearings; one makes the round,
checks bilges, chain linkage, hold; gear aloft, alow.
The voyage is ended, the gales and storms endured
are done, the ship lies easy in the sheltered bay,
having made her passage and come to rest.
Don't think her safety's even once assured.
The vigil's to be kept all night and day,
the anchor's holding always under test.

The Ship Sings

The ship sings—she can't whistle.
That right is to and only to the cook.
At the waterline the surging waters rustle.
In low voices the mate and helmsman talk.
Twilight's given way to fog; the night
and darkness reign, the off-watch sleeps
snug in their canvas cradles, lullabyed
by pulsing engines, rocking on the deep.
Aloft, the wind plays and strokes at chords
in the taut lines, but the real music's
heard in measured choruses from the hold, the play
of plank-on-plank and beam-on-bulkhead creaks
keening as the bowsprit rises toward
heaven on the swell, then falls away.

Graveyard Watch

This night at its darkest positively glows.
A calm sea throws back a milk-lit sheen.
The helmsman, red eye on the compass rose
confirms his wind on cheek. A dim starboard green
lights slack clews. Benched on skylights forward,
the bow watch peers into nothing. The jibboom's fall
rises, a shadow on the sky. Even the figurehead
is half-asleep, nodding over the blue-pale
phosphorescent whitecaps before a low wake.
Alongside, a whale blows unseen. Overhead
the forecourse, wanting a breeze, slats aback.
Fog banks, the stars go out; bow watch spells
the helm. "East by south" the only words said
until the night watch ends. Eight bells.

Part Four: Navigation

The Sextant

The sun you have with you always, whether its light
illumines day, or its absence promises dawn.
Nothing is more sure than that the night
follows day and its meridian.
"Never look straight at the sun," but yet
the sextant's use requires that you must.
Having done this before it begins to set,
one's latitude may be truly known, not guessed.
If chronometer has kept pace with that unseen
tick of seconds we call time, and if
we understand and read the tables true
to chart where we are now, and where we've been
on this wide and vacant sea, it is enough.
We know as closely as we'll ever know.

The Binnacle

On blue water, the ship's *here* and *now*
and track abroad on the globe's wide and empty span
may be read from these: star, sun, compass.
This last took ancients' lodestone and centuries to refine
by slow measures—Kelvin's balls, Flinders' bar,
charted variation, swung ship, rose and lubber's line—
until, brass-bound, lamplit, coupled to a star,
the binnacle emerges, bright Venus from the brine.
It's an alchemists' dream realized, perpetual motion
(one moving part, albeit slow) in *this* machine.
It can (corrected for compass error) show
the ship's course on the trackless ocean.
Thus we measure what is never seen
and understand what we can never know.

True North

Out of sight of shore, the sun rises and sets
his daily round over the changeful face
of the boundless deep. The landed world forgets
how one cloud's like another, how a new place
on the ocean's like the last. At sea, we steer
by star and compass, by instinct. The binnacle light's
a comfort, but the needle's set to bear
on a false north. Still, through darkest nights
the helmsman keeps the course—he must.
An order's not a matter for understanding,
it's not a matter of choice to obey.
The captain's skill has earned the owners' trust
to bring ship and cargo across oceans to a landing,
but it's the true and unseen force that shows the way.

Celestial Navigation

The mate logs the place and time of Altair's rise.
Forward, the tropic heaven's milky stream
just illumines the sea to the lookout's eyes.
Above, the brighter, nameless stars and planets gleam.
The helmsman keeps his eye on one beside
the main course weather yardarm. It is
on this clear dark night as true a guide
as the dim-lit numbers on the compass rose.
Our place among the fixed stars does not change
as night after night each one assumes its place
right on schedule, in steadfast relation.
Study them well; these bright points, with undying light
secure our place in all of God's creation,
though storm and cloud obscure them for a night.

All the Seas of the World Are One Water

We shape the water with our hulls, it shapes
us in turn—spring, river, history and font—
calls our commerce past the stormy capes
from port to port. Tide and unseen current
mingle all the waters, sweep around the curled
horizon. In all our discovery, we've merely named
ancient truths long abiding in the world.
Waves beat the shore beneath our awkward steps,
upwelled from depths beyond our little reach.
In time we learn to swim across the rip
like that first creature, to walk up on the beach,
and from that landing, like sand and ashes scatter
to be washed homeward, seaward, to become
with all the seas of the world, one water.

A note about the author:

David Hirzel was born in Philadelphia, raised in West Virginia, and landed in northern California by way of Florida. Today he makes his living designing energy-efficient housing for the future. He writes from Sky Ranch overlooking the Pacific Ocean in Pacifica CA. Extensive research for his nonfiction narrative series on the Antarctic explorer Tom Crean led him to the historic ships at San Francisco's Hyde Street Pier where he now leads the volunteer Living History Program. Two works in the series— Sailor on Ice: Tom Crean with Scott in the Antarctic 1910-1913 and Hold Fast: Tom Crean with Shackleton's *Endurance* 1913-1917 are available in print and digital formats at www.amazon.com. The third in the series, Tom Crean with Scott's Discovery Expedition 1901-1904 is slated for release in 2015. Additional works include the online podcast audiodrama Sailor On Ice (at *http://imaginationlane.net/tomcrean/*)

The poems in this book were written on board, or after sailing on the tall ships *Robert C. Seamans* and *HMS Bounty,* and the catboat *Kitty Sark.*

Front cover photograph: *Bounty* Sails, by David Hirzel
Back cover photograph: David Hirzel aloft on *"HMS" Surprise*, by Alice Cochran

www.ingramcontent.com/pod-product-compliance
Lightning Source LLC
Chambersburg PA
CBHW060623070426
42449CB00042B/2480